T0081149

# Agricultural DRONES

by Simon Rose

Consultant:
Todd Golly
Chief Operating Officer/Founder
Leading Edge Technologies

CAPSTONE PRESS
a capstone imprint

Edge Books are published by Capstone Press,
1710 Roe Crest Drive, North Mankato, Minnesota 56003
www.mycapstone.com

Library of Congress Cataloging-in-Publication Data
Names: Rose, Simon, 1961- author.
Title: Agricultural drones / by Simon Rose.
Description: North Mankato, Minnesota : Capstone Press, [2017] | Series: Edge books. Drones. | Includes bibliographical references and index. | Audience: Age 8-14. | Audience: Grade 4 to 6.
Identifiers: LCCN 2016023851| ISBN 9781515737674 (library binding) | ISBN 9781515737759 (pbk.) | ISBN 9781515737957 (ebook (pdf)
Subjects: LCSH: Aeronautics in agriculture--Juvenile literature. | Drone aircraft--Juvenile literature. | Agriculture--Remote sensing--Juvenile literature.
Classification: LCC S494.5.A3 R67 2017 | DDC 631.3--dc23
LC record available at https://lccn.loc.gov/2016023851

**Editorial Credits**
Carrie Sheely, editor; Steve Mead, designer; Tracey Engel, media researcher;
Katy LaVigne, production specialist

**Photo Credits**
Alamy: © 67photo, Front and Back Cover, blickwinkel, 11, Chris Biele, 12–13; AP Images: Ng Han Guan, 24; Getty Images: Kathryn Scott Osler/The Denver Post, 15, Bloomberg/ Michael Nagle, 19; iStockphoto: Onfokus, 8-9; Newscom: Mike De Sisti/TNS, 20–21; Shutterstock: Alexander Kolomietz, 28–29, Andis Rea, Design Element, Brothers Good, Cover and Interior Design Element, DamienGeso, Design Element, Eric Isselee, 16, Fotokostic, Cover Background, Kolonko, Design Element, Konstantin Ustinov, Design Element, Nik Merkulov, Cover and Interior Design Element, Mykola Mazuryk, Cover Background, Olivier Le Moal, 18, Pagina, Design Element, PointImages, 4–5, robuart, Design Element, Steve Collender, 6–7, TMsara, 10, Vjom, Cover and Interior Design Element; The Image Works: Kike Calvo/V&W, 23, 26; USGS, 17

# TABLE OF CONTENTS

# CHAPTER 1

# Solving a Mystery

A puzzled and worried farmer looks out over his field. He has a problem with his crops. Some of the plants are wilting and others are growing more slowly than they should. His fields are very large. He doesn't have time to walk through his fields and check the plants. The farmer isn't sure what is causing the problem. The plants could be growing in poor soil or have inadequate access to water. Diseases or pests could also be causing the problem. The farmer wants more information before deciding what to do.

Luckily, he has exactly what he needs in his barn. It is a small drone with rotors.

# FACT

Drones that fly are also called unmanned aerial vehicles (UAVs).

The farmer enters a flight path for the drone using his smartphone. He programs in the area of the field where the drone should take photographs and video. The drone flies on its own, but the farmer watches as it crisscrosses the field. After about 20 minutes, the drone returns to the farmer and lands. The farmer **downloads** the data from the drone to his laptop computer.

## FACT

Some drones can cover 200 acres (81 hectares) in about 20 minutes.

The farmer examines the images the drone's camera has captured. He zooms in on some images and sees evidence of pests on the leaves. He also notices dry patches in the soil where the plants lack water. The farmer now knows what he needs to do to manage his crops.

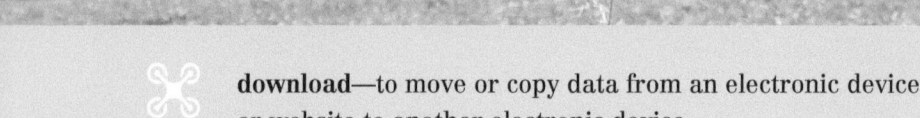

download—to move or copy data from an electronic device or website to another electronic device

# CHAPTER 2

# Eyes in the Sky

Agricultural drones have a lot in common with other UAVs. Like most other drones, agricultural drones are equipped with cameras, sensors, and **navigation systems**. But there are some differences. Agricultural drones are usually smaller than military drones or commercial drones used by businesses. They also carry less equipment and do not spend as much time in the air. Agricultural drones have the most in common with recreational drones that people fly for fun.

Agricultural drones are some of the most affordable drones. Advanced recreational drones might cost up to $5,000. Military drones may cost millions of dollars. A basic agricultural drone may cost less than $1,000.

## FACT

In the United States most crops are on farms that have at least 1,100 acres (445 hectares).

A man inspects his onion crop with a Typhoon Q500+ drone.

## Many Uses

Drones can be helpful to both crop and livestock farmers. Crop farmers use agricultural drones to **survey** fields and sections of crops. Companies that provide crop surveying services to farmers also use these drones. Livestock farmers use drones to monitor the health of animals and track their movements.

**navigation system—** equipment that allows a vehicle to follow a course from one place to another

**survey—**to look over and study closely

## Advantages of Agricultural Drones

Why use a drone? The advantages are numerous. Farmers and ranchers often have very large properties. It can be difficult to travel long distances to manage animals or crops. Drones

can save travel time and expenses by checking a farmer's property more efficiently. Drones can track animals' movements. They can check crops for signs of disease and pests. They can gather information on the number of plants and their heights. They also can show growing conditions, such as soil moisture. Some drones can even spray herbicides or pesticides to help crops grow. Herbicides kill weeds, and pesticides kill insects and other animals that can damage plants.

 plant showing signs of disease

An agricultural drone's camera is its most useful feature. These cameras take high-**resolution** images that have very clear detail. These photographs are less expensive to get than those taken by **satellites** or manned aircraft such as helicopters. Agricultural drones fly very low, so their cameras are unaffected by cloud cover.

**resolution**—describes a device's ability to show an image clearly and with a lot of detail; low-resolution images don't show as much detail as high-resolution images

**satellite**—a spacecraft used to send signals and information from one place to another

# AERIAL TREE SURVEYS

The high-tech cameras on agricultural drones can be useful for other jobs. In 2012 on the Kintyre peninsula in Scotland, a fungus called *Phytophthora ramorum* had spread from rhododendrons to larch trees. Thousands of trees had to be cut down to try to stop the fungus from spreading further. Forest managers there had a great idea. They decided to use drones to monitor the situation.

Drones took photographs of the forest's remote areas. Their cameras took close and detailed images of the trees and their leaves. These images helped forestry managers see when a tree was in the early stages of disease. The tree could then be cut down before the disease spread to other trees nearby.

 The Kintyre peninsula is heavily forested.

## Flying by the Rules

People who fly any type of drone need to follow rules. Countries make their own rules about drone use, although not all countries have drone laws. In the United States, the Federal Aviation Administration (FAA) sets rules for drone use. The FAA currently limits drone flights to a height below 400 feet (122 meters). The operator must be able to see the drone at all times. Drone flights are not allowed within 5 miles (8 kilometers) of airports without permission.

According to FAA rules, drones must operate in daylight. They can operate during twilight only if the drone has anticollision lights.

In 2016 the FAA changed it rules for drones weighing under 55 pounds (25 kilograms) for business purposes such as farming. People no longer need to get a permit for business use of drones. But operators do need to be at least 16 years old, complete certification training, and follow all FAA rules. Those without training may still fly if they are supervised by someone who has completed training.

# CHAPTER 3

# Drone Parts and Features

Although agricultural drones share some features, the technology in them varies. For example, an operator on the ground can control an agricultural drone with a **remote control**. The operator directs the drone to areas that need to be photographed. Some drones can also fly by themselves on a preset flight path. Farmers must match the drone's technology with their individual needs. The more technology a drone has, the more it usually costs.

## Wings and Rotors

Most agricultural drones have either fixed wings or **rotors**. Fixed-wing drones look like small airplanes. They can cover a wider area than rotor drones and fly for longer periods of time. Fixed-wing drones also can carry more equipment and collect more information quickly in one flight. They are usually more expensive than rotor drones. Farmers often use them to take scans that can be used to make a **3-D** image of a field.

remote control—a device used to control machines from a distance

rotor—a set of rotating blades that lifts an aircraft off the ground

3-D—having or appearing to have length, depth, and height

maneuverable—able to move and control easily

A technician assembles a fixed-wing drone at agricultural drone manufacturer Agribotix in Boulder, Colorado.

Rotor drones operate like small helicopters. They use rotors to fly. Multirotor drones have more than two rotors. Drones with four rotors are called quadcopters. Rotor drones are more **maneuverable** than fixed-wing drones. They can hover over certain parts of a field and fly closer to the ground than fixed-wing drones. They also need less room to take off and land.

## Cameras

Agricultural drones can carry different types of cameras. **Thermal** cameras detect plant and soil heat. Plants that are **dehydrated** will give off more heat than plants that have enough water intake. Farmers can use this data to create a map of the field that shows areas of increased heat.

**Near-infrared** cameras can help show plant health and **chlorophyll** levels. Healthy plants reflect near-infrared light differently than unhealthy ones do. When a plant becomes dehydrated or sick, the plant doesn't reflect as much near-infrared light. The healthy plants then show up in a different color on the image than unhealthy plants.

RGB cameras capture images with very accurate colors. This helps farmers assess the health of plants by studying the color of their leaves.

## FLYING HERDERS

In 2015 an Irish farmer used a small drone to herd a flock of sheep between different fields. The drone's camera helped the farmer make sure that no animals were lost. The sheep responded to the drone, which may mean that local border collies may one day be out of a job!

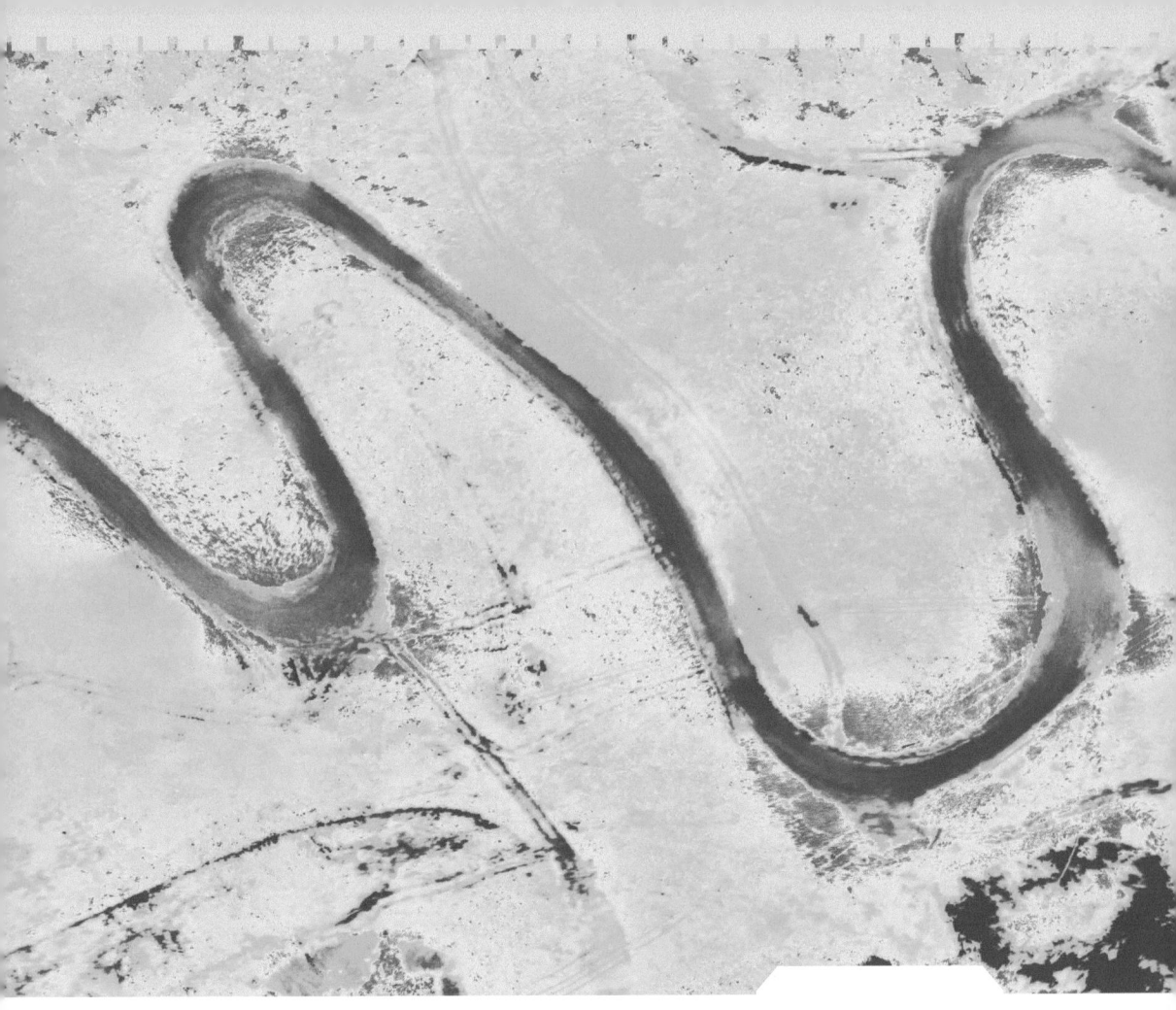

🔬 Data from near-infrared cameras can be used to create maps of fields. In this image the red areas show healthy plants. The blue areas show less healthy plants.

**thermal**—having to do with heat or holding in heat

**dehydrated**—not having enough water

**near-infrared**—related to short wavelengths of radiation that are not visible to people

**chlorophyll**—the green substance in plants that uses light to make food from carbon dioxide and water

## Agricultural Drone Sensors

Sensors on drones measure things that are not normally seen. For example, accelerometers sense movement or vibrations and keep a drone stable when it is flying. Some drones are equipped with thermal sensors that can detect an animal's temperature. This helps a farmer know if any livestock have a fever. Some drones can even detect weather conditions such as high winds. High winds can make a preprogrammed flight too difficult for a drone. The drone can then automatically return to base.

## FACT

In 2014 the company Stevia First made plans to fly drones with LED lights over stevia crops at night. The leaves of stevia are used to make artificial sweeteners. The LED light helps the plants produce their sweet ingredient more quickly. The company began its flights near Sacramento, California.

Workers assemble a drone at a manufacturer in Brooklyn, New York. Workers carefully assemble drones to be sure the sensors and other parts work properly.

## Bodies and Motors

Drone bodies are made from light composite materials such as **carbon fiber**. Composite materials are as strong as metal but weigh much less. These materials are often used in spacecraft and other aircraft. Composite materials reduce a drone's weight and give it more maneuverability.

Agricultural drones have battery-powered electric motors. The type and size of battery determines how long the drone can stay in the air. Most agricultural drones stay in the air less than an hour before needing to be recharged.

## FACT

Shake, shake, shake, and fly! To start the motor of the eBee agricultural drone, the operator just shakes it three times. Then the operator simply throws it into the air.

In 2015 British company Intelligent Energy invented a way to extend drone flight times. It added a **hydrogen** fuel cell to the regular battery. By doing this, a small drone was able to fly six times longer. Agricultural drones may use this technology in the future.

A pilot tests an agricultural drone in Mazomanie, Wisconsin.

**carbon fiber**—a strong, lightweight material made with acrylic fiber using high temperatures

**hydrogen**—a colorless gas that is lighter than air and burns easily

## GPS

Drones are equipped with **Global Positioning System** (GPS) navigation systems. GPS uses a system of satellites orbiting Earth. The satellites work together to pinpoint exact locations on Earth's surface. A GPS receiver communicates with the satellites to tell a drone operator exactly where the drone is on its flight path.

Using GPS, a farmer can plan a drone's route to only fly in a certain area of a field. He or she can set the route so that the drone flies around obstacles. Some drones can be programmed to return to their takeoff locations. The farmer can then pick up the drone after its flight.

## FACT

Some researchers are building agricultural drones with robotic arms. These drones could someday pick pests off plants.

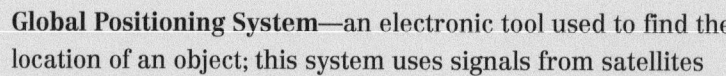 **Global Positioning System**—an electronic tool used to find the location of an object; this system uses signals from satellites

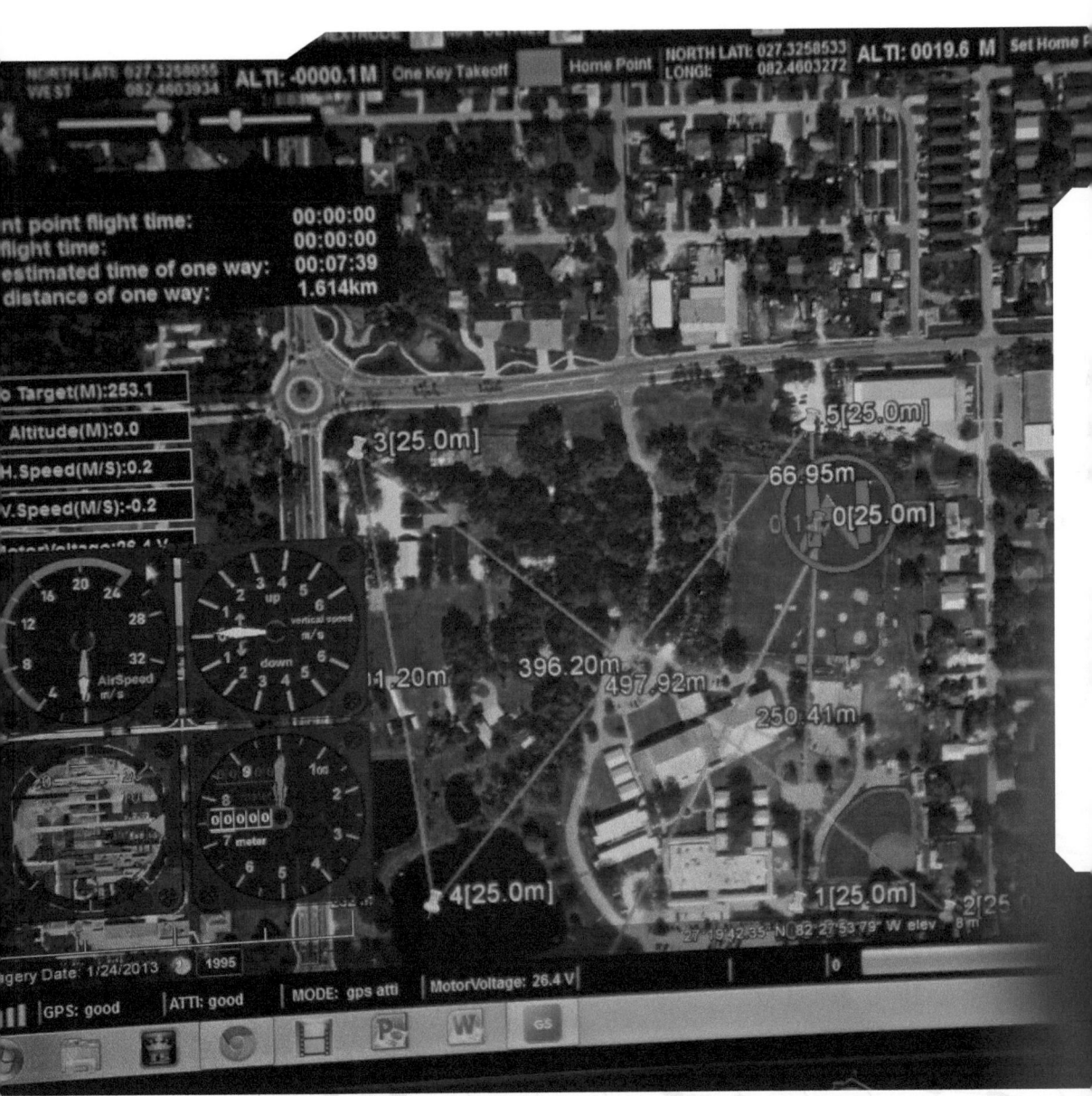

An operator can easily set a preset flight path for a drone by looking at a map on a screen. The operator can then choose places for the drone to fly.

# CHAPTER 4

# Flying into the Future

Experts believe that drone use will expand around the world in the coming years. Most of these drones will be small machines such as the ones used by farmers. The FAA estimates there will be at least 7 million drones flying in the United States by 2020. Of the drones purchased for business use, more than 80 percent are likely to be used in agriculture. According to the FAA, recreational and commercial drone sales are expected to rise from 2.5 million in 2016 to 7 million in 2020.

An agricultural drone flies over a field in China in 2015. It is demonstrating how drones can be used to spray pesticides.

## Reasons Behind Drone Expansion

What are the reasons behind increased drone use? One big reason is the improving technology of drones. Drones are not only becoming smaller but also cheaper. This means that even more farmers will be able to afford them.

For some countries, other factors could contribute to an increase in agricultural drone use. Japan's population is aging, and many of the country's rice farmers are elderly. Fewer young people are interested in working in agriculture. Drones can help fill in for fewer workers. In China the drone industry is booming. The government promotes the use of modern farm machinery, including drones.

## FACT

Some farmers think of creative ways to use their drones. In Suffolk, England, a farmer is using his drone to scare away pigeons from his crops. This helps keep the pigeons from eating his crops.

🔅 Locals of Nepal, Asia, learn how to fly a drone during a humanitarian workshop in 2015.

## Feeding the World

The United Nations predicts that Earth's population will be 9.7 billion by 2050. If everyone on the planet is to be fed, improvements need to be made to agriculture. Drones can help check the amount of water in the soil and monitor plant health. In turn, farmers can make the best use of their water resources and use fewer chemicals.

The population is expected to increase the most in developing countries. Better food production in these areas could help sustain the population increases. As drones become less expensive, more farmers in developing countries may be able to buy them. A group of farmers in these areas could buy one drone and share it.

# SOME OF THE LEAST DEVELOPED COUNTRIES

The United Nations keeps track of which countries in the world are least developed. Africa currently has the largest number of countries on this list. This chart shows some of the least developed countries as of May 2016.

| COUNTRY | GEOGRAPHIC AREA OF WORLD |
|---|---|
| Burundi | AFRICA |
| Niger | |
| Madagascar | |
| Zambia | |
| Malawi | |
| Eritrea | |
| Nepal | ASIA |
| Bangladesh | |
| Afghanistan | |
| Myanmar | |
| Solomon Islands | AUSTRALIAN COAST |
| Haiti | CENTRAL AMERICA |

## More Drones and New Laws

Governments will likely need new drone laws as more people use them. These laws can help prevent collisions between unmanned aircraft and people, power lines, and other aircraft. Some agricultural drones also carry dangerous chemicals that might hurt people or animals if the drones crash.

More laws could also help protect the privacy of the public. Some people do not want drones with cameras to fly over their private property. Without privacy laws, an operator could use a drone to secretly spy on the property of a neighboring farmer.

Agricultural drones are a huge help to farmers around the world. Laws guiding drone use will help ensure that drone use can continue to expand.

Lawmakers are still exploring privacy laws for drones in the United States. Current FAA laws address safety concerns for drones more than privacy concerns.

# GLOSSARY

**3-D**—having or appearing to have length, depth, and height

**carbon fiber** (KAHR-buhn FY-buhr)—a stong, lightweight material made with acrylic fiber using high temperatures

**chlorophyll** (KLOR-uh-fil)—the green substance in plants that uses light to make food from carbon dioxide and water

**dehydrated** (dee-HY-dray-tuhd)—not having enough water

**download** (DAUN-lohd)—to move or copy data from an electronic device or website to another electronic device

**Global Positioning System** (GLOH-buhl puh-ZI-shuh-ning SISS-tuhm)—an electronic tool used to find the location of an object; this system uses signals from satellites

**hydrogen** (HYE-druh-juhn)—a colorless gas that is lighter than air and burns easily

**maneuverable** (muh-NOO-ver-uh-buhl)—able to move and control easily

**navigation system** (NAV-uh-gay-shuhn SISS-tuhm)—equipment that allows a vehicle to follow a course from one place to another

**near-infrared** (NEER-in-fruh-RED)—related to short wavelengths of radiation that are not visible to people

**remote control** (ri-MOHT kuhn-TROHL)—a device used to control machines from a distance

**resolution** (re-zuh-LOO-shun)—describes a device's ability to show an image clearly and with a lot of detail; low-resolution images don't show as much detail as high-resolution images

**rotor** (ROH-tur)—a set of rotating blades that lifts an aircraft off the ground

**satellite** (SAT-uh-lite)—a spacecraft used to send signals and information from one place to another

**survey** (sur-VAY)—to look over and study closely

**thermal** (THUR-muhl)—having to do with heat or holding in heat

# READ MORE

**Faust, Daniel.** *Commercial Drones. Drones: Eyes in the Skies.* New York: PowerKids Press, 2016.

**Marsico, Katie.** *Drones.* Engineering Wonders. New York: Children's Press, 2016.

**Scholastic.** *Drones: From Insect Spy Drones to Bomber Drones.* New York: Scholastic, 2014.

# INTERNET SITES

FactHound offers a safe, fun way to find Internet sites related to this book. All of the sites on FactHound have been researched by our staff.
Here's all you do:

Visit *www.facthound.com*

Type in this code: 9781515737674

 Check out projects, games and lots more at **www.capstonekids.com**

# INDEX